Dennis Wheatley and the (
(an essay concerning a writer and

Craig Cabell

Bellack Productions

An Account of a Writer and His Research

Craig Cabell's revered chap book of Dennis Wheatley's research into the occult has been available online for many years; but only available in print as a signed limited edition leather-bound book, until now.

Fully revised and illustrated, and complete with actor Christopher Lee's special Introduction from *The Devil Rides Out*, *Dennis Wheatley and the Occult* is finally available in Trade Paperback.

Read about the men of power Wheatley came into contact with and how they convinced him, through their dark works, never to meddle in Black Magic, a message he told the world with conviction.

Dennis Wheatley and the Occult
(an essay concerning a writer and his research)
by

Craig Cabell

For Peregrine Solly, for his wit and companionship

Contents

The bookplate of Dennis Wheatley

Acknowledgements

I would like to thank the great Christopher Lee for the interviews and permission to use his special foreword to *The Devil Rides Out*. Thanks are also due to Peregrine Solly for the laughter, lunches, companionship and introduction to Dominic Wheatley. My thanks also to Anthony Wheatley. A thank you to Brian Aldrich who accompanied me to my first interview with Christopher Lee and got some much-prized photographs – enjoyed to this day. Thanks to the former celebrity book seller Nigel Williams who provided some much-needed inspiration and some rare Wheatley acquisitions, which really helped my research for this book. Simon Gosden and Fantastic Literature for his help in finding some out of print Wheatley-related books. My father Colin for his early thoughts and, of course, the great Dennis Wheatley himself, for his great stories and a little bit of magic when I most needed it.

CC

Dennis Wheatley

Dennis Wheatley and the Occult
(an essay concerning a writer and his research)

Craig Cabell

'Towards the end of 1968 I at last received an offer for the film rights on two of my books. Christopher Lee, unknown to me, had long been a fan of mine and was pressing Colonel Carreras of Hammer Films to make *The Devil Rides Out*.

Christopher took the part of the Duke de Richleau and played the role magnificently. Another factor which led to the great success of the film was that the script-writer stuck, as far as film technique permitted, to the story.'

The Time Has Come… The Memoirs of Dennis Wheatley – 1919-1977, Drink and Ink
Dennis Wheatley

A signed photograph of Christopher Lee in the Hammer
movie version of Wheatley's *The Devil Rides Out*

Foreword
By
Christopher Lee

I first met Dennis Wheatley approximately twenty-five years ago in the book department at Harrods. He was giving a lecture, which was extremely well attended, on the subject of 'Magic and the Supernatural' – on which of course he was an expert. He made it eminently clear during this lecture, as indeed he has in all his books, either as a preface or in the course of the book itself, that when White Magic becomes Black Magic and the occult and supernatural are used as a means of serving Satanic forces, they are immensely dangerous to the mind and soul. As he said many times to me in conversation, Dennis had never participated in any ceremony of any kind, being only too well aware of the great dangers involved. His knowledge was therefore based on a great deal of reading over the years and on many conversations with people who were scholars or writers like himself. Through their knowledge of the 'left-hand path', as it is so often called, they were able to affirm how desperately perilous is any study or practice of this Art.

I introduced myself to him after he had given the lecture as someone who had read all his books many, many times and as someone who was absolutely fascinated both by what he had to say and by the manner in which he presented his stories. He was graciousness itself to me and we had a conversation which lasted for about fifteen minutes. At that time I could only speak to him as someone who was a great admirer of his work, and as an actor who had appeared in a fair number of films. To the best of my knowledge, Dennis' books on the occult and on Satanism had not been transferred to the screen to any great extent, so I remember asking him if I had his permission to approach a film company with regard to the production of one of his books for the screen. He very kindly said that I had *carte blanche* so to do.

Some years later – I think I'm right in saying it was about 1967 – I finally convinced Hammer Films, with whom I had already a close association, to make *The Devil Rides Out* – probably his most famous book of its kind. For many years it had been extremely difficult for any film company to take the risk of presenting this particular subject on the screen. I think probably this was because of the religious involvement concerned. As it happened, the established Church, indeed the various religions, were only too pleased to have this kind of material filmed, because it clearly demonstrated what an appallingly dangerous thing the practice of Black Magic and Satanism is to the very existence of the soul.

The film was made and was a great success. I am informed that it was presented in the USA under the title of *The Devil's Bride* because some executive genius in the distribution company concerned had said that if it were to come out under the title of *The Devil Rides Out*, the American public could conceivably think it was a Western. No comment necessary. It appeared in this country and in many others under its original title, and in America and possibly in other countries with the alternative version. I am happy to say that Dennis was extremely pleased with the result, and I am fortunate enough to possess a first edition of *The Devil Rides Out* signed by him with a very kind comment in terms of the film and, indeed, my performance as the Duke de Richleau.

Of course, Dennis Wheatley was considerably more than an immensely popular and widely known storyteller. It is common knowledge that he was involved in many different jobs in his lifetime before he became a writer – amongst them that of wine merchant. I know from personal experience, having been to his house many times, that his knowledge of wine was encyclopaedic and his generosity to his guests was unlimited. Furthermore, during the Second World War Dennis worked in Top Secret Intelligence deep in the bowels of Whitehall, and his contributions to the Disinformation Campaign – of such vital importance to the invasion of Europe by the Allied Forces – was of great significance. I believe he was involved in the extraordinary story of The Man Who Never Was, which of course is now well known to hundreds of thousands of people, and also in the equally important invasion of Western Europe under the heading of Operation Fortitude. It was he and many like him who, as a very closely knit group, were able to spread false invasion rumours which penetrated the very highest levels of the German command, and led to the saving of literally thousands of lives.

Dennis was a very dear friend of mine and my family's. Always generous, always kind. I remember once when he invited me to lunch at the St James's Club, as it was then called, in Piccadilly, that he turned up wearing a teddy-bear coat and a white Homburg which at the time I said made him look exactly like Al Capone. He roared with laughter. He loved the absurd and was a man with enormous humour and great warmth, as all his friends will agree. He was also a man who really loved life. An inveterate traveller. Whenever I met him he'd always been to the ends of the earth for some reason or another and he and his wife, Joan, were global travellers in every sense. I don't think there was anywhere in the world that Dennis hadn't visited at one time or another and of course what he saw, what he heard and what he learned became of enormous importance in terms of the books that he wrote.

He is, I suppose, best known for his books on Black Magic, and rightly so, because nobody has written on that subject with such a universal, popular appeal. At one time he was good enough to say to me that I could have the rights to any of his Black Magic novels for nothing. What generosity! Unfortunately, for one reason or another, I was never able to mount a production which would do justice to the other books in this particular genre. Some, of course, would be prohibitively expensive even to this day. Others would require very complicated special effects and, indeed, rather complicated scripts. But I've always regretted that, of all the marvellous books that he wrote on this subject, we were only able to present two. (I know of course that many of Wheatley's books were turned into films before 1967.) The second of Dennis' films which was made by Hammer was *To the Devil a Daughter*. I was very disappointed in the result. So was he. I remember saying at the time that there were certain things in this film – particularly during the last five minutes or so – which did not represent the intentions of the author or, indeed, make any kind of sense in terms of a story. I didn't think that the appearance of a somewhat obscene rubber doll was appropriate and I certainly didn't think that my own particular death – or 'disappearance' – was very successful in view of the fact that, as one critic mentioned, it would be straining the bounds of belief to suggest that the Devil could be dismissed by being clunked on the head by a rock. Or in this case a piece of flint. There was another ending shot in which I, as the renegade Satanist, attempting to follow Richard Widmark and Nastassja Kinski through an astral gale, was halted by divine intervention and destroyed when further attempting to cross the circle of blood. I thought this was rather good and appropriate as the priest concerned fell over backwards in a position of crucifixion, which was an obvious allegory. For reasons of their own, with which I never agreed at the time and still don't agree, the producers decided otherwise. Consequently, after being struck on the head, I literally vanished from the scene. I think it was this, plus one or two other points in the finished film, that Dennis found inappropriate. I can only say that I entirely agreed with him.

However, I do know, because he told me himself, that *The Devil Rides Out* was his own special favourite. Watching it the other evening on television I found myself thinking that, good as it was, if we were able to do it with the special effects available today, it would be quite stunning and would have an even greater impact. After all, we're talking about a difference of twenty-one years and the enormous advances made in the cinema technically and photographically would, I think, justify another production of the same story.

Above all, I am very grateful to have known and to have called Dennis Wheatley a friend. When I read his books I am always amazed at the depth of the background information contained therein. It is customary of course for an author to do his homework and to fine-tune his research, but Dennis – not only in his books about Black Magic, but also in his books about the Second World War with his character Gregory Sallust – somehow makes you feel when you are reading that you are actually in the room, privy to everything that is going on and living the story literally as he describes it. I personally would very much like to make many more of his books into films and so many would warrant this.

It's many years now since he left us, but I never look across from my own home towards the house he lived in without thinking of him – and that's nearly every day. I shall always remember the meetings we had, the meals, the bottles of wine – superb of course – that we shared together. To me he is in the line of the great romancers like Arthur Conan Doyle, like Rider Haggard and many, many more. But whereas they perhaps invented a great deal of their subject, Dennis did not. He was very well aware of what he was writing about and, in the case of his books about the supernatural, equally well aware of the dangers involved. I think that all those people who might for one reason or another be inclined to participate in any kind of ceremony belonging to the Other Side, have probably been saved from committing the ultimate folly by reading his books. For my part, I as an actor always tried to present the concepts of Black Magic and Satanism for the true horrors they are. I remember once being approached by an Irish bishop in the street near where I lived – which was only a hundred yards from Dennis own home. He said that he and his 'flock', as he put it, were enormously impressed by the films because of course in the end, quite rightly, Evil is vanquished and Good triumphs. This, I am convinced, is what Dennis Wheatley was trying to show.

This Foreword was first published in the Century Hutchinson edition of *The Devil Rides Out* in June 1988, and used by kind permission of the author Christopher Lee.

Christopher Lee, star of *The Devil Rides Out* a
photographic study by Brian Aldrich

'… the majority of people go past the doors that are half ajar, thinking them closed, and fail to notice the faint stirrings of the great curtain that hangs ever in the form of appearances between them and the world of causes behind.'

The Insanity of Jones
Algernon Blackwood

Dennis Wheatley and the Occult
(an essay concerning a writer and his research)

'There is a "gap in the curtain" through which some people can see. Of that I have incontestable proof.'
'Foretelling the Future'
An article by Dennis Wheatley, reprinted in the revised 1963 edition of his anthology *Gunmen, Gallants and Ghosts*

Between January 1933 and November 1977, Dennis Wheatley reigned as one of the most popular horror/thriller writers in the world.

He confessed that during one forty-eight hour period, without sleep, he wrote twenty thousand words, drank several bottles of Champagne and smoked two-hundred cigarettes. He was a most dedicated writer.

There are few scholarly works within the horror genre, as the science used there-in is often too speculative to be taken seriously. When a balance between fact and fiction is achieved, a classic horror novel is born. In Bram Stoker's *Dracula*, there is the presence of the (then primitive) science of blood transfusion and the sound reasoning of doctors, one with a conventional opinion (Dr Seward), and one with a more eccentric approach (Dr Van Helsing).

Stoker maintained a keen balance between the two doctors, keeping the story within believable parameters (that's where the story succeeds). A similar trait can be found in Robert Louis Stevenson's *Strange Case of Dr Jekyll and Mr Hyde*, one-and-the-same character (Jekyll and Hyde) provide the extreme parameters on that occasion.

A first edition of *The Devil Rides Out*

In 1935, Dennis Wheatley took the Black Art of the occult and constructed a plausible story around it. With *The Devil Rides Out*, Wheatley took the hard research of a taboo subject and made it accessible to the general public. He did it well. Not only did he convince his readers that devil worshippers lived in modern-day society but they posed a very real threat too.

During the past decade, I have met several men who knew Dennis Wheatley personally[1], and each one has

---

[1] Christopher Lee, Douglas Reeman (aka Alexander Kent), Frederick Forsyth.

said a similar thing: Wheatley was a lovely man but believed that he had come too close to the powers of the occult and that he was forever damned as a consequence.

In his Author's Note to *The Devil Rides Out*, Wheatley stated: 'I desire to state that I, personally, have never assisted at, or participated in, any ceremony connected with Magic – Black or White.' Never before had Wheatley spoken to his audience so directly. It was as though he had witnessed a satanic ritual himself and, in order to exorcise it, he wrote a fiction where good transcended evil. Wheatley had researched the occult quite thoroughly and was concerned by his finding; as he stated in his Author's Note: 'Should any of my readers incline to a serious study of the subject… I feel that it is only right to urge them, most strongly, to refrain… My own observations have led me to an absolute conviction that to do so would bring them into dangers of a very real and concrete nature.'

One does get the impression – through reading the above quote – that the research Wheatley conducted for *The Devil Rides Out* was enough to attract evil in a tangible form.

So what did Wheatley discover during his research for *The Devil Rides Out* (and maybe his other occult novels, such *as To the Devil – A Daughter, The Haunting of Toby Jugg* and *Gateway to Hell*)?

'I had been reading books on ancient religions and occultism for the best part of twenty years when I decided to write my first novel with a black Magic theme, *The Devil Rides Out*.'
The Devil and All His Works

Rollo Ahmed

Wheatley had seen enough of the occult to want to refute his own psychic ability. Actor Christopher Lee confirmed this point to me by stating: 'He (Wheatley) was convinced that he was cursed.' This 'awareness' started from the early to mid-1930s; around the time of researching and writing *The Devil Rides Out*.

People who dabbled in the unseen were attracted to Wheatley. In an article dealing with the occult, 'The Black Art and the Supernatural' (see *Gunmen, Gallants and Ghosts*), Wheatley wrote the following: 'Perhaps the most interesting man I met while collecting data for my novels with occult backgrounds was Mr. Rollo Ahmed. He was an advanced practitioner of Yoga and made good use of it. Although a native of the West Indies he never wore an overcoat and used to go about London in the winter in a thin cotton suit. One night, when it was well below freezing, he arrived to dine with me. He had no gloves but his hands were as warm as toast.

'Rollo Ahmed was deeply versed in Magical lore and possessed the gift of explaining it with great lucidity. From him I learnt much of the theory of the Black Art. Briefly it may be defined as a system of short cuts to obtaining Power.'

Although this isn't an example of Dark Power, Ahmed did inspire Wheatley to write in the same article: 'Anyone can say prayers, or think evil. God will give new strength and fortitude in answer to prayer. The Devil will give strength and resolution actually to perform the evil deed contemplated. However, the human brain resembles a radio set. It needs tuning in to get the best results.'

Wheatley's mind was tuned in from the outset of the 1930s – on becoming a writer – as he explained in yet another article concerning the occult, 'Foretelling the Future' (see *Gunmen, Gallants and Ghosts*): 'In the 1920s I used occasionally to visit a seer named Dewhirst. He predicted to me the circumstances in which I should meet my wife and even described the way she did her hair.

'In 1932 I went to see him again. Immediately I entered his room he exclaimed: "You've written a book!"

'That was pretty staggering as I had not seen him for two years and I had only just sent the manuscript of my first novel to an agent.'

Dewhirst gave Wheatley more information and this is where things began to get quite interesting, as Wheatley wrote: '... he went on: "You are on the right road at last. Someone whose name begins with H will sell millions of your books. They will be read in every country under the sun." Then he named a date, seven weeks ahead, on which I would have good news about my book.

On that date I learned that Walter Hutchinson had taken *The Forbidden Territory* for publication.'

Hutchinson would remain Wheatley's publisher for the next fifty years, selling an estimated fifty million copies of his works worldwide. There was a lot to be said for Dewhirst's powers. But all this is not to say that Wheatley's mantra was to write about the occult because, quite simply, it wasn't. He started out writing adventure stories, plus one non-fiction (*Old Rowley: A Private Life of Charles II*), before starting work on *The Devil Rides Out*.

In April 1934, Wheatley and his wife Joan, returned from a tour of South Africa. The result of this holiday would be Wheatley's novel *The Fabulous Valley*, his fourth adventure story. However, it was on the completion of this book that he turned to the subject that had intrigued him for neigh on twenty years – the occult. We have ascertained that by 1934 Wheatley had developed an interest in the occult, so did he decide to write a book concerning its powers and satiate his intrigue? Possibly, but he would conduct his research a little too well and put himself in an uncomfortable position. On more than one occasion, he invited Men of Power to dine with him at his London home, overtly building a level of trust that could, of course, be misconstrued. He was the perfect host, offering the finest food and wine. But who were the occultists that visited him? More importantly, how dangerous were they? Did they attempt to draw him into the Secret Art?

And did he witness anything – even as a casual observer – that would give him an absolute conviction of satanic danger? Well, nothing so dramatic – to begin with. One of Wheatley's first dinner guests was Harry Price. Price was not an occultist; he was a ghost-hunter.

His case study on Borley Rectory – the most haunted house in England – had won him much respect in his field and, to this day, his researches into the paranormal are highly praised.

It hung in the air like a brick don't – spooky goings on after the fire at Borley Rectory

Wheatley was fascinated with the prospect of life after death. He was convinced that the spirit lived on after the body had been exhausted and he was fascinated by his conversations with Price.

The first edition of *The End of Borley Rectory* in its rare dustwrapper

But Wheatley's guests would soon become more sinister. He got too close to dangerous men, such as the Reverend Montague Summers. Although Summers dressed as a clergyman, he had apparently been defrocked, or had never taken the holy orders at all.

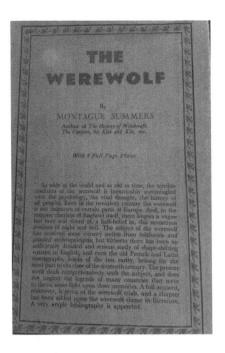

A very rare first edition of Summers' The
Werewolf in its original dustwrapper

Summers invited Wheatley and his wife to stay at his
country house – Alresford – for a weekend. The
incidents that occurred there are not fantastic in any
way, but when placed together are quite unsettling.

The Wheatley's arrived one Friday afternoon
and was shown around the grounds. Joan immediately
spotted an enormous toad sitting in the garden, nothing
too unsettling, but when they entered their bedroom,
large spiders scuttled across the ceiling, and the
Wheatleys began to feel quite unsettled.

If it was Summers' aim to shock or test his
guests, it certainly worked. But soon the visit took a
turn for the worst. That Saturday morning, Summers
asked Wheatley to accompany him to a large room that
was empty except for a pile of books. It was here that
the reverend would show his true colours. He picked up

a small leather bound volume and said: 'Look, this is just the thing for you. It is worth far more, but I'll let you have it for fifty pounds.'

Wheatley never disclosed what the book was, but it was obviously an instruction on the black mass (a more generic book on the occult could have fitted nicely into his collection). Wheatley declined the offer, saying that he couldn't afford it and, even if he could, he didn't want it anyway. He explained what happened next in his book *The Devil and All His Works*: 'Never have I seen a man's expression change so swiftly. From benevolent calm it suddenly became filled with demonic fury. He threw down the book and flounced out of the room. An hour later I had sent myself a telegram. By Saturday evening my wife and I were home again in London.'

One does tend to speculate as to what happened in the hour between Summers throwing down the book and Wheatley sending himself a telegram. However, it is clear that Summers misinterpreted Wheatley's intentions. His quest for knowledge would not progress into a practical study of the occult. If he had been tempted in any way, he would have surely accepted Summers offer. By the same token, Wheatley's experiences over that weekend did not deter him from exploring the subject further. His next visitor was the aforementioned Rollo Ahmed, whose own thirst for information on satanic rituals took him to the little explored forests of Yucatan and Brazil.

But going back to Summers. What impression did he leave on Wheatley? Summers was an occult scholar who edited 16th Century books concerning the occult (which were later published by the Folio Society), but despite this flirtation with society, Summers possessed power himself and this is what scared Wheatley, as the novelist explained in his article 'The Black Art and the Supernatural': 'The Reverend Montague Summers told me of an exorcism he had performed in Ireland. He was called to a farmer's wife who, it was said, was possessed by an evil spirit. He arrived in the evening. On the table in the living room the remains of a cold leg of mutton had already been placed for supper; the women was in the same room. At the sight of a priest she became so violent that she had to be held down. As he sprinkled the Holy Water on her and commanded the demon to come forth, a small cloud of black smoke issued from her foam-flecked mouth. It went straight into the cold mutton, and within a few minutes everyone present saw that the meat was alive with maggots.

'Few men had more knowledge of the occult than Montague Summers, and his books upon Witchcraft and Werewolves are classics. But he was, to say the least of it, a curious character. Rumour has it that he was not, in fact, a priest... With his long silver locks and, normally, benign expression, he looked like a Restoration Bishop. Years later I used his physical appearance for Canon Copely-Syle in *To the Devil – A Daughter*. For that I had a precedent, as in Mr Somerset Maugham's early book *The_Magician* the sorcerer, Hado, bears a striking resemblance to Aleister Crowley.'

Indeed, Crowley provided the inspiration for the main character in *The Devil Rides Out*. While researching the novel, Wheatley invited Crowley to dine with him to discuss the occult (Wheatley was introduced to Crowley by a journalist friend, a man who would later become a well-known member of parliament. A man whose identity Wheatley protected for many years), as he explained in his article 'White and Black Magic': '(it was) Aleister Crowley, who once assured me that it is perfectly possible to raise – he did not say the Devil, but that was what he meant... it is not suggested that the mighty Lucifer... appears to people in person. But each of us have a Guardian Angel, and it is his opposite number, a creature of the Devil's charged with our undoing, who, in exceptional circumstances, may become visible to human eyes.'

Aleister Crowley

In *The Devil and All His Works*, Wheatley tells us that Crowley was a wonderful raconteur and that he learned much from him concerning the black mass. Crowley even presented him with a signed copy of his book *Magick in Theory and Practice* (1929), which became a much prized possession in Wheatley's book collection[2].

Crowley's interest in the occult stemmed from his days as an undergraduate at Cambridge. He became an integral part of the Order of the Golden Dawn. Other notable members were Algernon Blackwood and W B Yates.

Crowley fell out with one of the principle members of the Golden Dawn MacGregor Mathers, and

---

[2] Wheatley included a plate of the signed title page in his occult non-fiction *The Devil and All His Works* (Hutchinson, 1971)

the two became deadly enemies. Mathers succeeded in getting Crowley expelled from the Order, whereupon Crowley formed his own, called the Silver Star. When Mathers died in 1918, many of his friends were convinced that Crowley had put a death spell on him.

After a few meetings, Wheatley was convinced that Crowley couldn't hurt a fly, but it was his journalist friend who told him that things were much different a few years previous. Crowley was never the same man after raising the horned demon Pan. He told Wheatley what had happened that night:

The ceremony was held in a small hotel owned by one of Crowley's disciples. The servants were given leave and Crowley and his coven moved in. The ceremony was held on a Saturday night. A large room at the top of the hotel was emptied of all furniture and vigorously cleaned.

Crowley's disciples waited downstairs under the instruction that whatever sounds they heard during the ritual that under no circumstances could they enter the room before daybreak.

At midnight, the interior of the hotel became intensely cold. Violent shouting and banging could be heard from upstairs but none of the disciples dared to investigate. The following morning, all was quiet. Crowley's disciples congregated outside the upstairs room. They called out but there was no answer, so they broke the door in.

What they saw was horrific. Crowley's son – who had performed the ritual with him – was dead, and Crowley was a gibbering idiot crouching in the corner. Before he was fit again, Crowley spent the next six months in an asylum outside Paris. Wheatley didn't laugh off this story, because his friend told him that indeed he was himself one of Crowley's disciples that dreaded night (Wheatley gives a pretty clear interpretation of the story – albeit in a fictional sense –

in his chapter 'The Black Art' in his novel *To the Devil – A Daughter*).

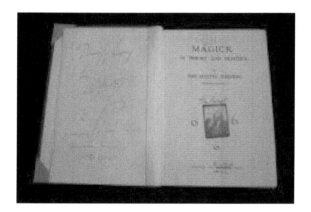

Wheatley's signed copy of Magick

Wheatley was told another interesting story by his friend: Crowley held a Sabbath when he was at Cambridge. Apparently, he was a brilliant scholar and planned to produce a Greek play; but owing to its immorality the Master of John's forbade him to do so. To be avenged he made a wax image of the Master, and then induced some of his fellow students to accompany him one night to a field. Having performed certain rites, Crowley called on the Devil and was about to plunge a needle into the liver of the wax figure; but his companions panicked. His arm was jerked and, instead, the figure's ankle was pierced. Next day the Master fell down some steps and broke his ankle.

'He tossed his head with the old arrogant gesture. "Little fool, your persistent blindness to my power becomes almost amusing... I, the Great Ram, am not as other men..."'
The Satanist

By the mid-1930s, Wheatley knew of the Powers of Darkness and didn't want to invite its influence any further into his life. The public loved *The Devil Rides Out* and his publisher pushed him to write more occult fiction; but he declined, most strongly when it came to occult non-fiction.

Wheatley's decision not to write an occult non-fiction during the 1930s is telling in itself. Also, for him to only write approximately a dozen occult related novels in a body of work in excess of seventy titles is again, telling to say the least.

Wheatley's only sin was conducting his research a little too thoroughly and leaving himself open to contact with men he should have kept at arms reach – if not further. After the publication of *The Devil Rides Out*, many people – from different walks of life – wrote to him, either praising him for the warnings he gave the reader in his book, or to give him more 'information' about the occult. He admitted this in his introduction to the short story *A Life For a Life* in his anthology *Gunmen, Gallants and Ghosts*: 'This macabre piece is the direct result of *The Devil Rides Out*... for years, after its appearance I had the most amazing mail about it from readers all over the world... Quite a number of writers covered many pages in a curiously similar type of scrawl which, after a time, I came to recognize as indicating that my correspondent was a mental case, whether certified or not. One gentleman signed himself "The Christ"... and wrote to me frequently for a long time giving the most fantastic explanations of the Book of Revelations. Another advanced the interesting theory that, the worship of Christ having failed to stop wars or materially to improve the conditions of the human race during the best part of two thousand years, it might not be a bad idea if we transferred our allegiance to the Devil and gave him a chance. The author of this original idea was actually an inmate of Broadmoor.'

Wheatley's short story *A Life For a Life* was inspired by a letter from a middle-aged lady, who intrigued him so much, he couldn't resist meeting: '(she) offered me data of such intriguing nature that I could not resist the temptation to break off my work one afternoon for the purpose of meeting her.

'The woman claimed that in the Essex village where she was born her grandmother had been a well known witch. When she was very young her father had sold her to the Devil. She had not realized that until many years later when, after a violent quarrel with her elder sister, that sister had accused her of being "Devil's Spawn" and in support of her accusation, recalled a scene of her childhood to her in which her father had opened a vein in her arm and made her scrawl her name on a piece of parchment in her own blood. As she grew up she had found to her alarm that she had the power to bring accident and ill-fortune to people by merely wishing them bad luck; she also developed second sight and could induce manifestations such as wall-rapping. To her distress, all animals were terrified of her and she had never been able to keep a pet. Strangest of all, it was impossible for her to go into church without being physically sick.'

Wheatley was deeply intrigued by this woman's story, as he explained: ' I am convinced that there was nothing whatever evil about her but it certainly seemed that she was a *focus for evil* and she spoke of her sad fate with such simple candour that I found it extraordinarily difficult to believe that she was romancing deliberately... in the space of some two hours, she told me many episodes from her supernatural experiences which were entirely in keeping with occult tradition and the details of which could only have been invented by a master of the subject. She did not attempt to borrow money from me, to enlist my aid in the publication of literary work or to persuade me to give a talk on "Ghosts" to some club or society. She came only to beg me to continue to warn people in my writings of the ghastly death-in-life which might overtake those who attempted to peer behind the veil. Finally she described to me in a rather hesitant way but with great vividness a dream which she had had on several occasions and of her conviction that one night this "vampire of the tomb" would overcome her and that she would be found dead in bed in the morning.

'She said that, if I liked, I might use the idea as the basis of a story... May God have mercy on her Spirit.'

'Suddenly an utter silence beyond human understanding descended like a cloak and closed in from the shadows that were all about them.'
The Devil Rides Out

While speaking on a BBC literary programme in the early 1960s, Wheatley stated: 'My background comes largely from very extensive reading over many years, but before I started with *The Devil Rides Out*, I secured introductions to many famous occultists... They convinced me that dabbling in the occult can lead to lunacy.'

Wheatley had a healthy appetite for the occult. He didn't 'dabble' in the Black Art himself, however he did everything but do it. He met men of power, who by their very nature, vindicated Wheatley's fears of supernatural danger.

' "Have you ever dabbled in the occult yourself?"
"Yes, in my youth... But I had an experience that convinced me that I was playing with fire..."'
The Used Dark Forces

If Wheatley ever dabbled in the occult during his youth is unclear. If the above quote from his novel *They Used Dark Forces* is autobiographical in any way – as some of his analogies were – then we would have to say yes, but we have little evidence.

But what are the facts about his youth – Wheatley's personality? Let us take a look and try to understand his young mind and its dark side. This is quite essential because quite simply, as Andre Gide states: 'One is always wrong to open a conversation with the Devil, for, however he goes about it, he always insists on having the last word.'

At the tender age of eight, Wheatley was considered a 'delicate' child. He was sent to boarding school in Margate. Since Victorian times, Margate was seen to possess health giving air, as it blows directly from the North Pole with no land intervening.

It was while at boarding school that Wheatley truly found his storytelling abilities: while enjoying midnight feasts and pillow-fights, he told his friends stories of pirates and highwaymen. Like a great many would-be writers, Wheatley fed the heroes of his stories with the strength and passion he so sadly lacked. The imagination of the young Dennis Wheatley had begun to take shape. He was living in a boy's own world and a natural progression from his stories of pirates and highwaymen would be headless horsemen, ghosts and ghouls. So Wheatley decided to expand upon these stories and this became his genesis as a writer.

The first part of Wheatley's autobiography (*The Time Has Come... The Memoirs of Dennis Wheatley – 1897-1914, The Young Man Said* 1977), offers us a little more to add to this genesis – a spooky story from roughly the same young age. As a child (aged nine), Wheatley – unbeknown to him at the time – saw a ghost whilst staying at a friend's house; as he explained: 'As the youngest boys, Bernie and I always went up to bed before the others. Our room was the first on the right on the first floor. One night we went up side by side, he on the right, I on the left, next to the banisters. There was no light on the landing but we could see our way by that which filtered up from the hall. When we were three steps from the landing I chanced to glance to my left. At that age my head came up only to the height of the banister rail. As I looked through the double row of banisters I found myself staring into another face within a few inches of my own. Beyond it was the dark outline of a man's figure. He was crouching low on the first few steps of the upper flight of stairs, and above his face one of his hands gripped the rail of the banisters. The face was round, white and horrible. I was petrified, struck dumb with fear, and remained rooted to the spot.

'Meanwhile Bernie had reached the landing. Opening the door of our room, he stepped inside and exclaimed, "Oh, what a lovely moon!"'

'The sound of his voice released me from my spell. Turning, I gave a terrified yell. As I plunged downstairs, I caught a last glimpse of the figure on the far side of the banisters. It, too, had turned. Swiftly and noiselessly it was gliding up the stairs towards the top floor.'

Wheatley raised the alarm that a burglar was in the house. His friend Bernie raced downstairs after him; but hadn't seen anything himself. On investigation, the adults could find no burglar either, and what with a thirty foot drop from the top floor to street level, it seemed either Wheatley's mind had been playing tricks on him or he had been witness to a paranormal experience.

During the Great War, Wheatley met an old friend (Milly Evans) who also used to stay at the same friend's house. During their conversation, Milly asked him if he remembered the fright he had given everyone by seeing a ghost? Wheatley politely informed her that he had never seen a ghost, whereupon she replied: 'Of course you thought it was a burglar. But it wasn't. I remember now that we let you go on thinking it was because we didn't want to frighten you further; but it was some sort of supernatural manifestation that you saw, and from the description you gave us, a pretty nasty one. The Hesters were very keen on spiritualism, and two or three evenings a week we used to practice table-turning, and that sort of thing. As nothing was taken and no man could have got out of that house without our finding some signs of his having been there, we have no doubt at all that our séances had attracted some form of elemental and it had begun to haunt the place. We were so scared that we gave up spiritualism.' Wheatley used this real-life story in his fiction *The Haunting of Toby Jugg*.

'"… it couldn't have been a man who had scared you… Naturally, as you were only a child, we concealed the truth from you and tried to make you forget the fright you'd had as quickly as we could. I don't mind admitting now that we were pretty scared ourselves, and I was thankful that we had already arranged to move from the Willows soon after Christmas."'
The Haunting of Toby Jugg

Although the sceptical would cast a rational thought or two over this story, Wheatley didn't, writing in the first part of his autobiography: 'In view of my complete ignorance of psychic matters at the age of nine, it is quite understandable that I should have taken a ghostly figure for a man of flesh and blood; and *the fact that I did* is irrefutable proof that I – the person who actually saw the ghost – played no part in establishing the intruder as a supernatural apparition. This personal and unsought experience has, in consequence, convinced me beyond all shadow of doubt that there are planes outside our physical world and disembodied intelligences which in certain circumstances impinge upon us.'

Signed First edition of *The Satanist*

Wheatley would back this statement up further by writing in his novel *The Satanist*: 'These psychic faculties came to us quite naturally. When young we accepted them as normal and made no special effort to develop them...'

If Wheatley was told of 'the truth' behind the story of the man on the landing (albeit during the Great War), then his mind had been certainly opened by the knowledge (placing the incident in a fictional setting in the late 1940s and then writing about it in the first part of his autobiography in 1977). Maturity had not dispelled the story – but there's something more. Something else happened to him during the Great War that would impinge upon his psychic abilities, as he explained in *The Devil and All His Works*: 'I do not regard myself as psychic but I have once felt that terrifying chill. I was building a shack by moonlight in an old walled garden behind the Somme battlefield (Wheatley received his first commission at the age of seventeen, in the 2nd/1st City of London Brigade R.F.A. he fought at Ypes and St. Quentin and in May 1918 was gassed and invalided home). It came upon me without rhyme or reason. I *knew* that something incredibly evil was watching me from behind – and it had suddenly become very cold. After a minute that seemed an eternity I panicked and fled in abject terror.'

In an article entitled 'White and Black Magic' (re-published in his anthology *Gunmen, Gallants and Ghosts*), Wheatley gave us another uncanny wartime story: 'As a young officer in the 1914-18 war, while convalescing I played a lot of *vingt-et-un*. After one ten-hour session, having become bored from drawing few cards worth betting upon… I called on the Devil to give me luck. I drew two aces, doubled the table, drew another ace, split three times and finished with two naturals and a five and under. Everyone paid me sixteen times his original stake. That shook the other chaps at the table; but it shook me infinitely more, as, sooner or later, that sort of "luck" has to be paid for.'

Ramsey Campbell, a respected horror writer himself, vindicated Wheatley's dread in *James Herbert, By Horror Haunted* (NEL 1992): 'Dennis Wheatley blamed everything that threatened his way of life on Satan.' Which beggars the question: from where did this fear stem? Indeed, what inspired Wheatley to call upon the Devil in the first place? I personally believe Wheatley was psychic, and therefore as Algernon Blackwood would state in his short story *The Insanity of Jones*: 'Adventures come to the adventurous, and mysterious things fall in the way of those who, with wonder and imagination are on the watch for them...' How do we know that Wheatley was indeed 'on the watch', as Blackwood puts it?

Algernon Blackwood

Frankly, we don't, however at the age of twelve he founded a 'Secret Society' and started writing papers that vindicated his boredom of the 'soulless place' he was living in. Unfortunately, some of these papers were found in his desk by his tutor and he was expelled from school as a bad influence.

As his imagination was taking on a fantastic and individual style at such a young age, it is reasonable to suggest that Wheatley's interest in the occult had begun, and could it be, by his rebellious nature, that he did dabble in the Black Art, just enough to scare himself from ever 'playing with fire' again?

If so, why would he return to researching a novel about it, collecting books and then writing a non-fiction some years later? Frankly, he probably wouldn't.

After being expelled from school, Wheatley was still a tear away. He became a cadet in the Royal Navy. Onboard HMS *Worcester* he would climb down a skylight in the middle of the night and raid the master's larder, roasting stolen potatoes in the hot ashes of the ship's furnace. He was always an adventurer, even though not physically strong. Chancing danger was always something he craved, so after acquiring an interest in the occult, he would push his luck to the limit in order to glimpse that forbidden world – but never dabble *too* much.

The success of his first occult novel would persuade him to write more, but as we have already discovered, he did not want to write a non-fiction on the subject. In fact, it took a lot of convincing on his wife's part to make him do that, but many years later.

But why? The answer lies in the mid-30s.

After writing *The Devil Rides Out*, Wheatley was indeed invited to write such a non-fiction book. He declined, advising his publisher that he didn't have sufficient knowledge on the subject to do so. He did however, put his publisher in touch with Rollo Ahmed, who did write the book (Wheatley providing the Introduction). The result was *The Black Art* (Hutchinson 1935). Wheatley loved the book and secured a copy for his own library.

Cloth cover to A Century of Horror, edited by Dennis Wheatley

Sadly though, Wheatley lost contact with Ahmed (rumour had it that he slipped up in a ceremony and failed to master a demon which had caused all his teeth to fall out).

Considering that the practice of witchcraft was banned up to the 1950s in Great Britain, Wheatley's grapevine for information appertaining to the occult was very good. Could this be another reason why he didn't want to write a non-fiction on the Secret Art? Did he feel that it might incriminate him or people close to him?

Probably not, as Wheatley did edit the acclaimed anthology *A Century of Horror* (1935), a book that ran to over one thousand pages in length. In his introduction, he spelt out his fear of the occult, obviously based upon his recent interviews with its practitioners: '... there is a very great deal of evidence to show that, given certain conditions, strange forces and evil powers from a world unknown – unknowable – can materialize in our atmosphere and strike stark ungovernable terror into the soul of man.'

'On that occasion I did not see anything at all. I only felt it; so the bigoted skeptic would be more inclined than ever to assert that my imagination was playing me tricks. I can only vouch for my belief that quite suddenly and inexplicably I found myself in the immediate vicinity of what I can but describe as disembodied evil.'
The Haunting of Toby Jugg

It wasn't until 1973, two years after the publication of *The Devil and All His Works*, that Wheatley agreed – with Sphere books – to release a series of occult reprints, including both fiction and non-fiction, under the generic heading *The Dennis Wheatley Library of the Occult*. Wheatley planned four hundred and fifty titles for this series, but unfortunately, less than fifty were actually published. His reasons for going ahead with the project gives weight to our reasoning so far: 'The literature of occultism is so immense that any conscientious writer can obtain from it abundant material... I have spared no pains to secure accuracy of detail from existing accounts when describing Magical rites or formulas for protection against evil, and these have been verified in conversation with certain persons, sought out for that purpose, who are actually practitioners of the art.'

It is clear what Wheatley intended with his *'Library of the Occult'*: to release a true all-embracing series of works that showed the true path of occultism; but what kind of information would these books contain?

'''He is a typical number eight person... They have deep intense natures and are often lonely at heart... and follow things through regardless of making enemies. It is not a fortunate number to be born under.'''
The Devil Rides Out

Writing throughout the night

What Wheatley ultimately wanted to achieve by meeting occultists, was verification on formulas and rites used in black ceremonies. He had so much information to hand he didn't really know what good advice was and what wasn't. One of the first formulas to be authenticated was the science of Numerology. It appeared in several of Wheatley best fiction, such as *The Devil Rides Out* and *They Used Dark Forces*.

Numerology had its origin in ancient Hindu; their priests were so far advanced they even understood the configuration of equinoxes (which are completed once every 25,827 years). The formula which Numerology is based upon is quite simple to understand: the sun, the moon and major planets in our solar system are directly associated with a number. According to *Cheiro's Book of Numbers*, the comparisons are as follows:

The Sun = 1
The Moon = 2
Jupiter = 3
Uranus = 4
Mercury = 5
Venus = 6
Neptune = 7
Saturn = 8
Mars = 9

Also, each letter of the alphabet is also associated with a number, as follows:

A = 1	F = 8	K = 2	P = 8	U = 6	Z = 7
B = 2	G = 3	L = 3	Q = 1	V = 6	
C = 3	H = 5	M = 4	R = 2	W = 6	
D = 4	I = 1	N = 5	S = 3	X = 5	
E = 5	J = 1	O = 7	T = 4	Y = 1	

It will be noted that no letter is the equivalent of 9. That is because in occultism 9 stands for the nine-lettered name of God; so no single letter could be ascribed to it.

By substituting numbers for letters in any person's name and adding them up, you arrive at their occult number, which is represented by a planet. That becomes a person's spiritual influence. The name used, must be the one the person is most commonly known by, even if it is an abbreviation or a nickname. For example, if a man called William is known as Bill, then his number formula will be calculated as follows:

B = 2
I = 1
L = 3
L = 3
_9_

By substituting numbers for letters, we find Bill's occult number to be 9, which gives us his planet number: 9 = Mars. If Bill was known by his full name of William, his number formula would look like this:

W = 6
I = 1
L = 3
L = 3
I = 1
A = 1
M = 4
_19_   1+9 = 10   1+0 = 1

When numbers add up to a figure greater than 9, the two numbers should be added together to obtain a number between 1 and 9. With William, we arrive at the number 19, so 1+9 = 10. Add together 1+0 you get 1, so William's spiritual planet is the Sun.

Naturally, a person's birth date will give the material number that governs a person's life. The material number is deemed to be more powerful; as it is a constant in a person's life (a name may be changed or altered in some way, most obviously through marriage).

The formula used for names is also used for birth dates. For example, if you were born on the 11th of the month $1+1 = 2$, and your material influence would be the Moon. If you were born on the 25th, then $2+5 = 7$, and your material influence would be Neptune.

People, who believe in the powers of Numerology, change their name to favour more positive planets. To see how you personally fair the basic table of planetary characteristics is as follows:

1. The Sun. Creative, inventive, strong personality. They are ambitious and usually successful. They resent restraint and are inclined to be obstinate, but they are good at wielding authority and earn the respect of those associated with them. They should endeavour to carry out their most important plans on dates having their basic number; and this applies to all other numbers.

2. The Moon. Gentle, romantic, artistic and have vivid imaginations, but they are not usually physically strong and often fail to carry out their ideas through lack of self-confidence. They are inclined to be over-sensitive and it is important that they should have cheerful surroundings, otherwise they easily become subject to depression.

3. Jupiter. They are lovers of order and discipline both in their work and in their homes. They are conscientious in carrying out orders but prefer to give the orders themselves. They are proud, dictorial and pig-headed, so are inclined to make enemies.

4. Uranus. Born rebels. Always take an opposite view to the generally accepted one, and instinctively react against all rules and conventions. They are seldom successful in worldly matters, but this does not greatly worry them, as they are much more interested in social questions than in making money. They are highly strung, inclined to feel isolated and do not make friends easily.

5. Mercury. They are quick in thought and action, detest routine work and love every form of excitement. They are great gamblers and often hit upon ways of making money quickly. They are liable to nervous breakdowns; but they have wonderful powers of recovery.

6. Venus. They possess more than the average magnetic attraction, so are much loved and often looked up to with devotion by those under them. They are inclined to be obstinate, but they become the willing slaves of people they love themselves. They like to see everyone about them happy, love beauty in all its forms, make lovely homes and are the art patrons of the world.

7. Neptune. They have independent and rather restless tendencies. They love all forms of change; travel as much as they can. They frequently make good writers, painters and sculptors, the sea being their most favourable medium; and, on it as sailors, or trading across it as merchants, they are nearly always fortunate; but they are not particularly lucky in money matters.

8. Saturn. They generally play some important role in life, but they are often misunderstood and suffer from a dealing of loneliness. They are inclined to be fanatical and sometimes appear

cold and indifferent to the opinion of others, but are actually warm-hearted. They are nearly always great successes or great failures. They should beware of forming any intimate association with a person whose number is 4, and avoid as far as possible anything connected with that number, as the combination of the 8 and 4 always beings misfortune.

9. Mars. Born fighters and make excellent sailors, soldiers and airmen. They are often called on to surmount difficulties in their early years but courage and a strong will nearly always brings them success. They are inclined to be conceited, resent criticism and tend to quarrel with their family. They have such a craving for affection that they can easily be made fools of by the opposite sex.

So here we have an authenticated formula, which Dennis Wheatley used in his books; but did he believe in it himself?

The answer is an emphatic yes.

Dennis Wheatley was born on 8 February 1897, and the number 8 in Numerology is an unlucky one to live with. But let us look at the breakdown of Wheatley's name via Numerology:

D = 4	Y = 1	W = 6
E = 5	E = 5	H = 5
N = 5	A = 1	E = 5
N = 5	T = 4	A = 1
I = 1	S = 3	T = 4
S = 3	14 = 5	L – 3
23 = 5		E = 5
		Y = 1
		30 = 3

$5+5+3 = 13 = 1+3 = \underline{4}$

Wheatley discussed this breakdown in *The Devil and All His Works*, vindicating his unqualified belief in Numerology and ostensibly, the occult: 'It will be seen that, if I were generally known by the whole of my name, I should be saddled with the unfortunate 4. This in conjunction with my birth number of 8, could prove catastrophic.

Fortunately, I never use my middle name... so my name as well as my birth number is 8.'

Wheatley went onto explain how dominating the number 8 had been in his life (a sample as follows):

1. Born on 8.1. 1897 = double 8
2. First big change in life: sent to boarding school aged 8 = double 8
3. Sent to the Western Front 8.8. 1917 = triple 8
4. January 1919. Entered family wine business at 26 South Audley Street. Number of shop and period of year = double 8
5. First marriage June 1924 at the age of 26 = 8
6. Second marriage 8.8. 1931 = double 8
7. Started to write at the age of 35 = 8
8. First book published January 1933 = 8
9. Moved in 1935 to 8 St. John's Wood Park = double 8
10. December 1941. Received commission in RAF and became member of the Joint Planning Staff of the War Cabinet. Age 44. Period of year and age = double 8

However, he dismissed all this with the line: 'Hundreds of people think of me simply as Dennis, which brings the resilient qualities of number 5 into play.'

'"But d'you see that the names Richleau and Ryn boil down to eight as well, linking us both with Simon. That's strange isn't it?"'
The Devil Rides Out

I believe that although Wheatley was proud of his success as a writer, he remained at odds with his occult fiction, as it was the key to the door of his own psychic abilities and, ostensibly, was a path he did not want to explore. Wheatley was very grounded, the papers he wrote during the Second World War for the War Cabinet prove this; they are methodical, logical and inspirational. He was indeed an old soldier himself and extremely practical. His common sense has left us all an important piece of advice concerning the occult: 'Should any of my readers incline to a serious study of the subject, and thus come into contact with a man or woman of Power, I feel that it is only right to urge them, most strongly, to refrain from being drawn into the practice of the Secret Art in any way. My own observations have led me to an absolute conviction that to do so would bring them into dangers of a very real and concrete nature.'

Wheatley knew that Black Magic was a serious religion, and not something to be taken lightly in fiction, that was why he wrote his in-depth study *The Devil and All His Works* at such a late stage in his career. He was always keen to tell the public that the threat of evil was a tangible in the everyday world.

Dennis Wheatley's final redemption came from his legacy – his constant preaching – to always tread the right path and not let evil enter one's life.

' "De Richleau was explaining the real horror of this thing to me last night. This promise of strange powers is only a filthy trap. At your first Christening your

Godparents revoked the Devil and all his Works. Once you willingly rescind that protection, as you'll have to do, something awful will take possession of you and force you into doing its will, an Earthbound Spirit or an Elemental…"'

The Devil Rides Out

Wheatley was very conscious of the Devil and his ways and found it his duty to warn people of his power. He was aware of his own involvement with the occult and kept this to a bare minimum. He summed this up at the end of *The Devil and All His Works*:

'It should be our aim to become conscious hedonists and derive pleasure ourselves from giving pleasure to other people. The only prohibition is that we should not gratify our desires if by doing so we are going to harm others.

　　　None of us can hope to lead perfect lives. But if we follow the right-hand path, we shall be armoured against the temptations of evil. We need have no fear of the Devil and all his works; *nor need the idea of death hold any terror for us*. With this thought I leave my readers.'

Dennis Wheatley was by default a custodian of White Magic, steering the average person away from the dangers of Black Magic and therefore cleansing himself of any dark force that conspired against him personally.

Epilogue
by
Anthony Wheatley

Dennis Wheatley died on 10 November 1977. Some days earlier, he was visited by his old friend, Cyril 'Bobby' Eastaugh, retired Lord Bishop of Peterborough. During the whole of their long friendship, going back more than fifty years, the Bishop had never ministered to him pastorally; but at this final meeting he did so and gave him conditional absolution. It is clear that this was not merely a courteous absolution. It is clear that this was not merely a courteous gesture to the religious susceptibilities of his old friend; because he subsequently wrote to another dear friend, Derrick Morley, saying how much he had appreciated Bobby's visit and that he felt at peace having received conditional absolution. It would therefore seem that he died a Christian.

The funeral service was conducted by the Bishop at Putney Crematorium; and, in accordance with his express wish, his ashes were buried at Brookwood Cemetary. The place is marked by a small tombstone, simply inscribed: 'Dennis Wheatley 8.1.97-10.11.77 "Prince of Thriller Writers" RIP.'

This Epilogue was first published in the final volume of Dennis Wheatley's autobiography *The Time Has Come... The Memoirs of Dennis Wheatley – 1919-1977, Drink and Ink* and used by kind permission of Anthony Wheatley via Dominic Wheatley of the Wheatley Estate.

Copyright Notices

Further Reading

Articles

Black Magic To-Day (article published in Daily Mail 10 October 1936 by Dennis Wheatley).

Dabbling With the Devil: The Real Danger (article published in Daily Express 27 March 1975 by Dennis Wheatley)

A Ghost Mr Wheatley Met On the Stairs (Sunday Express 9 January 1977 by Graham Lord)

That Satan Feeling (The Guardian 12 January 1977 by Raymond Gardner)

The Dean of the Occult (The Guardian 12 November 1977 by Alex Hamilton)

A first edition of Rollo Ahmed's *The Black Art* (John Long Ltd, 1936)

Non-Fiction and Introductions
The Black Art by Rollo Ahmed (John Long, 1936) (dedicated to and with an Introduction by Dennis Wheatley) (revised Jarrolds, 1968)
The Devil and All His Works by Dennis Wheatley (September 1971, Hutchinson)
Wheatley and the Flemings (And How They Lured Hess to Britain) by Craig Cabell (Bellack Productions, 2017)

Dennis Wheatley's Library of the Occult (vol 1 to 45) (Sphere Books 1974-1977)
The Time Has Come... The Memoirs of Dennis Wheatley – 1897-1914, The Young Man Said (Hutchinson 1977)
The Time Has Come... The Memoirs of Dennis Wheatley – 1914-1919, Officer and Temporary Gentleman (Hutchinson 1978)
The Time Has Come... The Memoirs of Dennis Wheatley – 1919-1977, Drink and Ink (Hutchinson 1979)

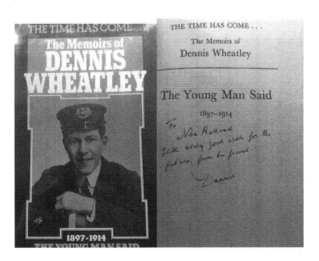

A rare signed copy of part one of Wheatley's autobiography, released the year the writer died.

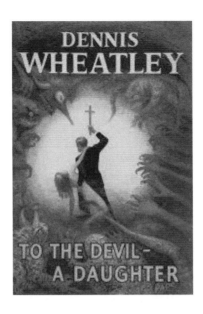

First edition of *To the Devil – A Daughter*

Selected Occult Fiction and Related Works
The Devil Rides Out (Hutchinson 1934)
Strange Conflict (Hutchinson 1941)
Gunmen, Gallants and Ghosts (Hutchinson 1943)
(revised Arrow Books 1963)
The Haunting of Toby Jugg (Hutchinson 1948)
To the Devil – A Daughter (Hutchinson 1953)
The Satanist (Hutchinson 1960)
They Used Dark Forces (Hutchinson 1964)
Gateway to Hell (Hutchinson 1970)

Christopher Lee and the author

About the Author

Craig Cabell was born and educated in South East London. He started writing commercially while still in secondary school. At the age of 13 he was a short story writer for radio. He became a freelance reporter shortly after leaving sixth form and the London College of Printing, writing most prominently for *The Independent* newspaper and the music press.

He was the Editor of the first Ministry of Defence (MoD) online news service and wrote extensively in-house for the MoD House Journal, before moving into other areas of government services, working in the Middle East and both South and North America. He was the creator of the industry-led Ballistic Toolkit and introduced the Nimbus non-lethal car protection system into Iraq.

His work as a biographer and historian started from the millennium, his second book, *The Kray Brothers – The Image Shattered*, is noted as one of the most accurate and respected books regarding Britain's most notorious gangsters, which was recently optioned for TV. He later produced another Kray book with former jewel thief Lenny Hamilton titled *Getting Away With Murder* and included contributions from Leonard 'Nipper' Read (the Krays' arresting officer).

Cabell's military history books, such as *Operation Big Ben, the anti-V2 Spitfire Mission 1944-45* (with Graham A Thomas) and *The History of 30 Assault Unit, Ian Fleming's Red Indians*, have been widely praised and copied, the former inspiring limited edition models and a short CGI movie, the latter inspiring the movie *Age of Heroes* starring Sean Bean and Danny Dyer.

Cabell's book of reminiscences to commemorate the 60th Anniversary of VE Day was used in a special celebrity gala performance in Trafalgar Square with

Richard E Grant acting out vignettes from the book and was re-issued to mark the 70th anniversary.

Over the past ten years his books for John Blake Publishing have include *James Herbert – Devil in the Dark, Ian Rankin and Inspector Rebus, Killing Kennedy* and the acclaimed *The Doctor's Who's Who*, featuring biographies and detailed film and TV guides of every single actor who has taken on the most famous role.

Cabell lives and works in London.

Books by Craig Cabell

Frederick Forsyth – A Matter of Protocol, the Authorised Biography

The Kray Brothers – The Image Shattered

James Herbert – Devil in the Dark, the Authorised True Story

Operation Big Ben – the anti-V2 Spitfire Missions 1944-45 (with Graham A Thomas)

VE Day – A Day to Remember (with Allan Richards)

Snipers (with Richard Brown)

Dennis Wheatley – Churchill's Storyteller

Getting Away With Murder (with Lenny Hamilton)

Witchfinder General – the Biography of Matthew Hopkins

Ian Fleming's Secret War – Author of James Bond

The History of 30 Assault Unit - Ian Fleming's Red Indians

Ian Rankin and Inspector Rebus

Captain Kidd (with Graham A Thomas and Allan Richards)

The Doctors Who's Who (Celebrating its 50th Year)

Terry Pratchett – The Spirit of Fantasy

Blackbeard (with Graham A Thomas and Allan Richards)

Killing Kennedy

Operation Big Ben – the anti-V2 Spitfire Missions (revised solo edition, 2016)

Iain Banks – A Tribute

David Bowie – A Tribute) (also exists as a colour illustrated special edition)

The Last Shot in Dealey Plaza

Chap Books by Craig Cabell
Dennis Wheatley and the Occult
Wheatley and the Flemings (and how they lured Hess to
Britain)
1.15-3.30: the Battle of Trafalgar
I Was Alive Then - the Spike Milligan Interviews
The Curse of the Baskervilles
A Spooky Thing Happened on the Way to the Keyboard
Operation 40 and the Big Event

Black Sniper (fiction)
On the Way to Dixie (fiction)
Words of a Free Spirit (fiction)
Happiness is a Warm Tome (fiction)
The Burning Man (fiction)
The Secret of Flat 35 (fiction)
Why Did I Invite Them Round to Tea? (fiction)
Knapswitch & Pucker (fiction)
Passing Strangers (fiction)

Children's Fiction
The Nan Who Fell to Earth (fiction)
The Dance of the Necromancer (a poem) (also available
as an extra illustrated colour special edition)
My Brother, the Mountain Beast

Audio Fiction
The Man Who Loved Christmas (fiction)
Guest House (fiction)
Night (fiction)
Akin to Light (fiction)
Mr Rake (fiction)
The Flame and the Whisper (fiction)

Special Introductions by Craig Cabell

Annabelle Says by Stephen Laws and Simon Clark
(Editor/Introduction)

*Furies Over Korea – the story of the men of the Fleet
Air Arm, RAF and Commonwealth who defended South
Korea, 1950-1953* by Graham A Thomas

Firestorm, Typhoons Over Caen, 1944 by Graham A
Thomas

*Terror from the Sky – the Battle Against the Flying
Bomb* by Graham A Thomas

The Dan Drown Enigma by Graham A Thomas

Writer Dennis Wheatley, who implored his readers to
never dabble in Black Magic

Printed in Great Britain
by Amazon